Th...
Pa...dise

The Life of Carolina Brooks

Carolina at the canal in French Harbour

Carolina Brooks
Cel/ 96666536

1

CAROLINA BROOKS

Compiled and Edited by Kendall and Harrison Johnson

<u>Forward</u>

Cruisers disembarking at the Port of Coxen Hole in Roatan

Dawn breaks and the ball of red lifts above the horizon, calling out a new day to the cruisers! The loud hum of treadmills fills the glass lined upper deck as the passengers madly combat the over indulgence of food consumed the day before. Lush green hills emerge to starboard eliciting a growing excitement for the day ahead. Ever gradually the ship maneuvers alongside one of the most beautiful sights in the western Caribbean, the stunning island of Roatan!

A luxurious breakfast and a checklist of 'what to bring' for a beach day precedes the herding off a gangplank to be greeted by a blast of furnace heat and colorful Garifuna dancers. Ushered into a cattle line for the awaiting Mercedes bus and accompanying jolt of satisfying air conditioning, the dancers amuse and entertain.

Whisked away past brilliantly colored wood homes, up a winding tropical forest road to impressive ocean vistas, and down again to an infamous stretch of crystal turquoise waters and blinding white coral sand, known as Tabyana Beach. Filled with envy at the 'local' owners sipping umbrella drinks, laughing at sailing stories and laying on padded loungers by the sea, the day begins ... ahhh this is PARADISE!

Unseen in this exotic and idyllic setting are the many hidden impoverished souls daily struggling for their very survival! Entrapped by the meager circumstances of life and the lack of resources that could elevate their existence, they plod along. Steeling themselves for each new dawn, barely hoping for a better tomorrow, angered at the barriers to the life of those cruisers, bored by the monotony, they rise amongst the stench of poverty and look to survive another day.

This is the reality for many on the wonderful island of Roatan! This, my friends, is The Darker Side of Paradise!

What you are about to engage in reading is the story of one of these souls. This is the real life of Carolina Brooks, as only she could tell it.

- Pastor Bob Cowan

Intro

Happiness: A feeling of pleasure, contentment or peace based on the quality of your surroundings

Most people take moments of happiness for granted. We enjoy an afternoon at the beach, lunch with a friend, holidays with family, or simply being at peace with the way things have turned out.

4

Worry, pain, and fear are the antithesis of happiness. These emotions destroy even a hint of peace and pleasure. While the world around us moves non-stop focusing on number one, there are millions of people who daily get left in the dust dealing with these temporary feelings that destroy their happiness. Most of them are able crawl out of the gutter but there are some who will never see the light. This story is real and not the normal bad to good, 180° plot line that readers crave. There are moments of joy, hope and faith throughout, but in Carolina's own words, "My life is pain; I've never known happiness." She has found joy in writing her life and I have found joy in walking with her through the process. I praise God for an amazing woman who has held on to her faith amidst a life of suffering and has been able to raise 5 boys to be educated men.

Carolina

My name is Carolina Brooks. I was born in 1962 in La Ceiba, Honduras but I have spent my life in Roatan. I am a true islander, raised up from a child. In this story you will get a picture of real life in Roatan. Tourists come to my island every day but they only see what the tour companies and the resorts want them to see. I will show you what happens beyond the tour bus and behind the resort walls. My life is pain. I have never known happiness for more than a moment.

I never really knew my mother or father; they both stepped out of my life very early on. When I was a little girl my mother's life began to be tough for her. Things went wrong and my dad beat her up a lot so she made the decision to leave and make a better life for herself. While I was still a little baby, she left me at the house with my grandmother and she went to find that better life. I heard later that she was in the United States but she never forgot about me. She wrote to my grandmother often to ask about me and to make sure I was doing fine.

When my mother got settled down she picked up a job and began to send my grandmother a couple dollars to help take care of me. Years went by without hearing my mother's voice and I constantly wondered what her life was like living in the United States. I dreamt about going to be with her, and living in a place where I was happy and loved by my mother but I knew better than that. I knew Roatan was my reality and I had to accept it.

We lived in a small village behind Hybur when I was a little girl. Hybur is a big shipping and fishing company on the island where many of the locals work. The boats come in and bring all their fish, shrimp and lobster there to be packed up and shipped around to different parts of the world. When I was growing up I used to love to be down by the water. I would go to bathe in the creek and I was able to leave everything behind. For a little while I was able to be a kid and play without worry or pain. Sometimes I would go to the creek all day from morning until night. One day I was bathing for hours until it was dark. I finally got out but I could barely walk and I had chills all over my whole body. I was scared and when I ran home with all the energy I had, my body felt like it was crumbling. My

6

muscles burned and I could not stop shaking. I was about 11 years old at the time when I was diagnosed with polio.

Medical help has always been hard to find on the island. Even today in 2011 people have to take a ferry to the mainland of Honduras for basic surgery. As I write this, my Aunt Gladys is sitting in the hospital waiting for the doctors to send her to the mainland because they cannot help her. Though it is hard to imagine, the hospital can't figure out her problem because they don't have the right equipment. She has a lump on her back, pain in her throat and has lost her voice. She will be sent to three different hospitals and won't receive proper medical care to remove the tumor for another three weeks. Everything is a process here; you learn to be patient from a young age. It is normal to wait five hours in a doctor's office or to wait days in the hospital to see a doctor for a minor treatment.

The hospital here was built in 1991, but by the looks of it you would think it was built in the 60's. There is one working toilet, unsanitary floors, second hand everything, 2 sinks, and you must provide your own toilet paper, clothes food and pillow.

Roatan's Public Hospital

The hospital wasn't built when I was diagnosed with polio but they took me to the best doctor on the island, Dr. Polo. He looked me over and decided he could not help me and said I needed to go to the hospital on the mainland. They rushed me to San Pedro Sula and the doctors did all they could, but the polio had already taken hold of me. My jaw was locked in place, one leg had contorted and was now shorter than the other and I had very little control over my legs and feet. I had to use my hands to hold my legs and make them move to walk. I wore pants all the time and would have to get a good grip of the fabric to lift one leg at a time, moving slowly and with tremendous effort.

I couldn't eat anything solid because my jaw was locked in a way that only left about a ¼ inch opening. I could only have liquids and things that could be eaten through a straw. I mashed or grinded everything and consumed all my meals this way. This was difficult but the most painful part of this was and still is my teeth. I was unable to brush my teeth because I couldn't fit a brush into the opening of my mouth. For seven years I did not brush my teeth! No one knows the pain I endured and still deal with to this day.

Every tooth rotted out and since then most have been removed. I still have one tooth in the back that is black, black, black and sometimes when the pain comes it hurts worse than you can imagine and it gets very swollen. It has been going on for years and it still hurts constantly. I only have three original teeth left and they are all rotten. My mouth doesn't open all the way so I have no way to get them out because the dentist cannot pull them. It's a problem I have that nobody knows about because I don't tell anybody my problems. They are my burdens and I don't want to worry people with them. I think God knows the reason why he has me hold on to those teeth. I don't understand why He makes me live with them so long, but I believe He has a reason for it.

<u>Overcome</u>

"Man needs difficulties, they are necessary for health"
-Carl Jung

I was raised with no love; I found love out there on the street. People that were not my family and not my color helped me find love. It may sound crazy but I am telling the truth.
-Carolina

After I was diagnosed with polio, we moved away from Hybur building to a place called La Loma or "The Hill" in a town called French Harbour. I was about 12 years old and I had not been to any doctors who could help me. I lived a long time in pain before I met the American doctors. We moved over to The Hill and my grandmother got a house. Up to this point in my life, I had never been to school but not because of my own choice; I wanted to learn. I asked my grandmother to enroll me and she refused, so I figured out another way. One of my friends checked me into school by pretending to be my mother. Somehow my grandmother found out and she did not accept it. Every time I would go to school she would beat me because she did not want me to learn. I kept asking why she didn't want me to go to school, but she never gave me an answer, only the back of her hand. My aunts and uncles couldn't read so my grandmother wasn't interested in me reading either. I was considered the black sheep of the family and she didn't want me to be educated if her own children weren't. Because of her own neglect and lack of upbringing, her children had never gone to school. She refused to allow me to have a leg up on her own kids. But she underestimated my passion and determination. I wanted to read and write and she wasn't going to stop me! I wanted to be something. People were always talking about us kids on The Hill saying, "That girl can't read, that one can and that one can but that one cannot." I wasn't going to be that girl. I was friends with a lot of white people who could read and I would be embarrassed to be around them because of this. I couldn't read or write and I was ashamed but I wanted to be educated like them. I was going to learn to read. My grandmother was not going to hold me down! She was just another hurdle I had to overcome.

It was hard to go to school with my friends because they would all be happy and making jokes, but I would be sad. They would ask me, "Carolina why are you sad?" and I would say, "Y'all are going home to be happy, I am going home to be beat." And it was real, it was just like I tell you, it was my reality. I would face that every day of my life. I decided to just accept it because I was determined to be somebody and not a dummy. I'd tell people, "Somebody is going to place a paper in my face one day and I am going to be able to read it. I am going to be able to write my own name and not have anybody write it for me." I continually told myself, "I will be somebody."

I now thank my grandmother for the beatings she gave me because sometimes challenges and difficulty make you want something even more. She would beat me and I learned in defiance. The beatings pushed me to study that much harder. My education was going to be worth the punishment. It was so hard for me but I had no other choice but to make it through so that no one would ever have to write my name for me.

When my aunts write a letter they have to give it to someone else to write and that's embarrassing, and looking back they are not to blame. My grandmother did not allow them the opportunity to learn, just like she didn't allow me.

I would not go home for hours after school because I dreaded the beatings. I didn't run away to places I wasn't supposed to be, I would go to my white

10

friends; they always welcomed me. They took care of me, fed me, clothed me and did anything for me. They loved me, something that was rare but cherished in my life.

Public School in French Harbour

Stand Up and Survive

When I was 14 years old I stopped going to school because I needed to work. I wish I could have gone further than fourth grade but I had learned enough and after my time in school, I continued to learn at home and on the street. At 14, I started working at a restaurant called The Yacht Club up on the Hill. Back then we still had no power on the island, so everything closed up at dark. I would serve the guests until about 5pm, and then I was able to go home. It was a good job but it was hard for me because I was waiting tables and I couldn't talk or walk very good.

The owners were nice enough but there was one time I had to stand up to the owner because she was trying to walk all over me. I figured out that when the customers would leave me a big tip on a table, the owner would walk by and snatch it up. I was so confused when I would go to the table and there would be no tip from some people I had worked hard for. So one day I got smart; I waited for a couple to leave and I watched from around the corner. As I stood there watching, my boss walked by my table and snatched up a good tip that was left for me. As soon as I saw that I walked out and accused her of stealing my money. She was so 'shamed' that she put the money right back on the table and didn't say a word about it again. I never lost my tips after that. Some people wouldn't have stood up to their boss like I did but I learned early on if you don't stand up for your own rights, no one else will and you will get walked all over. If you want something you have to do something about it and if you see something wrong, you should stand up for what's right.

One of my closest friends who always stood up for me is Mrs. Eleanor Bodden. She is like a sister to me. She lives in the states now, but every time she comes to the island, she comes to see me. Her family takes good care of me too by giving me what I need and showing me love. Anytime I would go to them in need, they were always there for me. Her mother is Mrs. Mabel Bodden, who has a heart of gold and cares for me like a daughter.

Mrs. Mable Bodden at her house in French Harbour

When I was about 16 or 17 Eleanor came and found me on the Hill. She was driving a nice new truck, which shocked me because I had never seen her driving anything. She said, "Come on Carolina, we are going for a ride." She was just learning to drive and wanted me to come cruise around the island in her family's new truck. We drove around for about 30 minutes feeling like we were on top of the world. We were making jokes about being famous and being the queens of Roatan. Not many people had cars on the island at that time so we felt like celebrities that day. But on our way back to the Hill something terrible happened. We were driving and all of a sudden Eleanor screams. She jerks the steering wheel to the right and my body flew to the middle of the truck. Next thing I knew we were upside down.

A child had run out in the road and Eleanor swerved to miss the kid. The bad part was that there was

13

a steep hill to our right, which led to the parking lot of the super market. When we turned down that hill the truck rolled a couple times and landed on its top. Eleanor's brother, had been in the back of the truck, and saw the accident coming. He was able to jump out of the truck before we started rolling. The car went down a steep hill and rolled over upside down. I was so scared and all I wanted to do was get out of that truck. I started beating the windows with my fist because I wanted out so bad. I wanted to break the windows and crawl out of there, but all Eleanor was worried about was me breaking her windows. Haha, she wasn't even worried about us. She was just screaming at me because she didn't want me to break the windows out of their new truck. We still joke about that to this day. The truck was all smashed up but she didn't want to lose those windows. People ran down to the Hill and told all our family and friends that we were dead, but someone helped us out of the truck and we walked home. Everyone was joking with us as we walked home saying that we were the walking dead. I believe God protected us that day.

Another special person in my life is Jerry Hinds. His family also took care of me and provided for me as I grew up. I always pray for God to give these families more because they treated me so good and loved me like a daughter. They use what God has given them to do good, so I pray for more blessings in their lives.

Jerry Hinds has been so special to me and I respect him like a father. I remember when he used to live in the house in front of a hotel called The Buccaneer. He worked real hard and used to pay rent for his mother. He would provide for his mother and the whole family. I would go by his house and they always had something to give me. They always had some food to give me or clothes or simply love. I constantly went to them for help and they never denied me.

Sometimes I would steal away from the Hill and go over by my white friends. That was my place where I would always go for peace. They treated me good, so that's where I went, to a place where I was treated like I mattered. People like Eleanor, Jerry, Mable and my other white island friends made my life bearable. They were blessings to me from God. My aunt beat me, my uncle beat me, everybody beat me, so I would steal away in the day and come back in the evening, spending as little time as I had to at home on The Hill.   I was unable to provide for myself, and no one in my family cared for me. It's like they had cast me aside, but I had made up my mind to survive. At that time, I was alone. I didn't have any kids at all, I only had to take care of myself but that would change soon enough.

"To whom much has been given, much will be expected."
-Bible – Luke 12:48

My Only Daughter

I had an uncle that lived in a town called Tela on the mainland of Honduras. He moved there when I was a little girl to find work, and no one had heard from him in years. When I was about 16 years old he came back to the island and showed up at my grandmother's house. He had been along with a Spanish lady in Tela for a while but they got in a fight and he left her. He had a little girl with him who was just a baby. My uncle claimed that the little girl was his and that she needed a mother. He said the Spanish lady he had been with was a bad woman and he didn't want to leave his daughter with a mother like that. So he brought her home to his mother, my grandmother, and then he disappeared again.

He left the baby girl and went back to his life without a second glance. I never saw him again but heard years later that he had been killed on the mainland. My grandmother had no desire to raise this child, so I became the permanent babysitter. There was no other option, the child had no one and no one wanted her. She was just like me.

People always took care of me because I couldn't care for myself. Now I had this child and I became like her mother. She had no one else and neither did I. I would notice many nights that my grandmother didn't have food for me nor her so I would pick up the baby, put her on my hip, and I would go by my white friends on the point. Cripple as I was, I had to provide. No one was going to come save us, so I had to survive and care for this child. The Bodden and Hind families would call us in from the street and feed us. They treated us good like always. I took care of the baby for years, cleaning her, feeding her, and begging for the two of us.

One lady who provided for us was Mrs. Francis Arch. She was a teacher and preacher in French Harbour for years and would always give us food when we were hungry. The baby was constantly getting dirty and I didn't have enough clothes to clean her up. We would go down by my white friends all dirty sometimes, which made me 'shamed, but we had no other clothes and no other option. I would go by Francis who had a big heart for that girl because she said the little girl needed a mother's love. She felt bad for me because I was still a child and was not fit to raise this little girl so she cared for us.

One day I went by Mrs. Francis' house and she said to me "Carolina, why don't you go ask your grandmother if she will let me have this baby girl and I will raise her." The Arch's didn't have any kids in the house anymore, they were all grown and I think Mrs. Francis missed having her kids around to care for. Her husband, Mr. Seth Arch, owned the dry dock where shipments came in. The Arch's liked the little girl and I knew they would love her well.

When I talked to my grandmother about this, she immediately cursed me out. I argued with her and told her that they feed us every day, they care for us and that I couldn't take care of this child anymore. I told her, "I can't mind this little girl when I need to mind myself. I can't walk good, I can't talk good and I got nobody to take care of me; just me myself." I kept repeating to her the same thing, hoping it would sink in and every time she would curse me. She had a deep-rooted bitterness toward the whites; I guess it was jealousy. But one day I think she finally accepted reality. I was not fit to care for this child and she sure didn't want the girl, so she agreed to give the little girl to the Arch's.

I don't know if she saw the Arch's as hope for the little girl or as an escape route for the two of us. Either way the girl was off to a better life and we were once again fighting only for ourselves. My grandmother knew the Arch's even better than me so she went to their home as soon as her decision was made. The Arch's told my grandmother how they took care of the little girl and me all the time, but they saw that I was not fit to take care of the little girl. My grandmother agreed and gave the little girl to Mrs. Francis.

That was a load finally lifted off my body and my mind. I felt so relieved; it was like somebody had carried my burdens away. The little girl was living like a queen now; she had everything. They put her through good schooling where she became educated and equipped for success. That little girl is married now, living in the States and has two kids. Her name is Norma Arch and for a little while I was the only mother she knew.

The Old Man

The message of Jesus:
Continuously make my sacrifice real by doing this very
thing, become broken and poured out for hopeless
people.
- Jen Hatmaker

Gringo*: A name given to foreigners in Latin America*
usually of North American or British descent. Folklore
says it was generated when the US invaded Mexico,
wearing green uniforms, and the people shouted at them
"Green Go Home".

      I was about 17 years old when the Gringo doctors came. They came to my island to help poor people with medical needs. There was one old Gringo man who had lived on the island for a long time and was always good to the people. His name was Mr. Bill. He was not a doctor, but he had a lot of doctor friends and he would recruit these groups from the States to come and help us whenever they could. I waited for hours to see the first group that came but they could not help me.

      Mr. Bill put me on a list and said he would have the next group that came help me out. Not long after the first group of Gringos left, the old man told me there was a group on the mainland and he wanted to take me to see them. This group was from Stanford University in California and they were helping people by giving them free medical care in La Ceiba. He had connections with them and he had promised me that we would go as soon as he could work out all the details. In a few days he got connected with the Stanford group in La Ceiba and told them my situation. They were moved with compassion and paid mine and the old man's passage on a plane to the mainland. At that time the flights were very cheap to La Ceiba, it would only cost us about $10 each to get there.

Mr. Bill set up the appointment with the doctors and flew with me over to La Ceiba so they could try to help me. The doctors that examined me were very nice, but they did not have the tools and materials to give me the kind of operation I needed. They said I needed brain surgeries, plastic surgery and surgery on my legs to give me back the life that had been taken from me by polio. They were unable to perform these surgeries anywhere in Central America and the Gringo doctors told me that I would need to go to the States for medical help. I had always dreamed of going to the States but I never thought it would be possible.

They made me a promise that very day. They told Mr. Bill that they would help me get to the States. I was a sad case and the doctors had compassion for me. I believe God brought them to me and me to them. They told Mr. Bill that they would get together some money and help set up the appointments if he could take care of the medical visa and all the other paper work.

I held onto that promise when I left La Ceiba. A lot of times people say things and make promises when they are confronted with suffering and poverty but then forget when they return to their own lives. Comfort and busyness can make you forget about pain in the world, but true compassion and commitment can change the world, or at least a life. The Stanford doctors did not forget about me. They sent some money to the old man and he was able to hustle up some other money from people he knew to take care of the flights and paper work. Once he had the money together, he took my passport and some other doctor papers over to the mainland. The day he returned he came and told me to get ready to go to the States. This was the most exciting day of my life. The old man had given me hope! He gave me a light in the constant darkness.

Everything was set up for me to go. The appointments had been made, the flights were booked and I had a place to stay in California. I will forever be grateful and indebted to the old man, Mr. Bill. He got everything together by himself for no other reason, but to show me love and that I was worth it. I saw all the work he was putting in and what he was doing for me so I wanted to do something for him.

I would wake up every morning and go clean up his house. It felt good to be able to give something back to him. It gave me a sense of dignity, something that had been gradually stripped from me over the years. For once I felt like I had value. Mr. Bill treated me good when I would come over. He always fed me and took care of me like I was his family. I respected him like a father because he was a good man and he treated me like a daughter. I liked to go by his house and work because I didn't want to be involved with all the problems over by The Hill where I lived. When I was working in his house I was in another world and I was worth something.

My grandmother didn't like it when I would spend my days at his house. She would make up lies and try to stop me from going. She would say that the old man didn't have respect for me and that he was taking me as his lady. She believed that he was taking advantage of me because she only saw me working for him for free. I would tell her what he was doing for me but she would say I was making up lies and living in a dream world. She didn't believe anything good could happen to me; she didn't think anyone could ever care for me. I was worth nothing to her, but I had hope. He was a good man with a heart full of love. I think he is dead now, I don't know, but wherever he is I know he has gone with God.

Mr. Bill helped people who were in the most need, which is where I believe God's heart is, 'with the least of these'. I believe when you do good for people with the most need, God blesses you more. That's where I was, I was desperate and he helped me. He got the visa and set up a foster family for me to live with in California. He would always mention a lady named Mrs. Amy who helped him with all of these things. This woman never knew me but was helping me all the way from the States and making sure things were going to work out for me; I know she has a good heart. He would get all of his information and help from her because she is very connected and well known in Stanford. I met Mrs. Amy one day, but it was years later back at home in Roatan.

Mr. Bill and the people at Stanford changed my life. I was living in constant misery and physical pain. I saw no way out for myself because I was so crippled but Mr. Bill gave me hope. I thought I was never going to go to the States but here I was ready to go; only a few more steps and I would be on my way.

Going Up

So I was finally ready to go to the States, the papers were ready and I already had my visa but we had one more hurdle. I was still a minor so my grandmother had to sign a paper that gave them permission to take me to the States and operate on me. Mr. Bill and one of my white friends, Mrs. Julie, went with me to talk to my grandmother about this. I knew that this was going to be a problem but my friends had no idea.

When we got there my grandmother listened as they carefully explained everything and then there was a pause. My grandmother looked at me, then back at them and said, "Over my dead body will I sign that paper! I'm not signing that fucking paper!" Mrs. Julie and Mr. Bill were a little shocked I think. But if they were scared by her, they didn't show it. They both stood there stone faced. Mrs. Julie asked, "Do you have a heart? Look at your little girl! She needs help and people are offering to give it to her." My grandmother responded by saying, "I wish Carolina would die!" After that, they took my grandmother inside alone to talk and had me stay out in the street.

When they came back after a little while, they had the signed paper in hand. I don't know what they said to her or if they bribed her in some way to get her to sign that paper but I am forever grateful for the way they stood up for me. I packed a small bag and we turned to leave. As we walked away from the house that day, I believed that I was leaving a part of my life behind and when I returned everything would be different.

We left and began our walk up the street to Mr. Bill's house and my grandmother yelled something from the porch that I will never forget. The words still ring in my head sometimes and it's like they are burning inside of me. She looked up at the sky and yelled at the top of her lungs, "I wish to Christ for that plane to crash and that only you would die!!!" I looked back at her in that moment and said, "Grammy, I am sorry for you. God don't hear those kinda prayers and I am going." I had my mind made up to live a little longer.

My grandmother was never there for me when I needed her. She was always turning her back to me, so when someone was giving me their front, I had to embrace it. I went from Honduras to California with a small back pack and a letter in my hand that would lead me to a new life.

Welcome to The Golden State

I arrived in California at about 2am and walked off the plane to be shocked by a chill I had never felt. It was January and I wasn't expecting this. Mr. Bill had told me it would be cold where I was going but I had

22

never known cold like this. Cold for me was an overcast 75 degrees during the rainy season. The temperature shocked my body and I began to shiver uncontrollably. As I walked out into the frigid night to wait for my ride, I could see smoke coming out of my mouth, something I had never experienced before. I was intrigued by it but not for long because my mind quickly went back to my shivering body and chattering teeth. Everyone that was standing around me was quickly leaving with family and friends who had arrived to pick them up but I didn't recognize nobody. I was scared and all alone.

I ran back inside of the airport and found a pay phone nearby. I dialed the number that Mr. Bill had given me in case of an emergency because I didn't know what else to do. He answered and I told him, "Nobody is here for me, everybody from the plane is leaving and I am still here." He said not to worry because some nice people were coming for me. I thanked him and I hung up the phone, still not feeling very relieved.

I remembered that I had packed a small jacket, so I dug to the bottom of my bag and pulled it out. It was old and worn out but for now it would have to do the trick. As I stepped back outside, I felt the cold bite me on the cheeks and again it took my breath away. I stood out on the sidewalk for a minute and noticed a white couple standing a ways away. They kept glancing over at me then whispering to each other so I thought that might be them. I didn't know what the people picking me up looked like but I knew they were clear skinned. We stood for a while repeating this exchange of looks and I began to be bothered by it. I was uncomfortable in this new place and just wanted to be somewhere familiar. I was starting to think this was a bad idea.

I wanted to walk over to the white couple and say, "What are you looking at me for, do I owe you something?" but I didn't say anything. I held my peace. The next time I looked over, the lady gave me a smile so I shared my smile with her as well. I guess she took that as a sign or something because she began walking over to me. She asked, "Are you Carolina Brooks?" And I said, "Why do you ask?" She then told me that her name was Mrs. Cathy and that they were the foster family I was going to live with in California. I was so relieved. I felt the pressure in my chest leave and the worry was gone. I told her, "I was so worried because I am in a new place and I didn't see anybody here for me. I don't know this place and for a minute I wanted to go back home." Mrs. Cathy looked surprised and said, "No Carolina, you know somebody. We are here for you and we are going to take care of you." She stepped close to me and hugged me up real good. She hugged me and loved me like I was family to her and we had just met. That's the kinda love I believe God told us to share with each other.

We drove for what seemed like hours, through the night and I was so exhausted, I slept most of the ride. Once we got to the house, all I wanted to do was sleep. Mrs. Cathy showed me to my room and I was shocked by the size of it. It was almost as big as our entire house in Roatan. This was the first time I had a room to myself or even a bed to myself. The room was beautiful with a big bed, a window that opened to the street below and bright yellow paint. I smiled and finally felt at peace, like everything was going to be ok.

I put on my night clothes and got in bed but I was freezing. I lay in bed and couldn't stop shaking; usually it's the opposite. At home in Roatan I would lie in bed every night and wake up in wet sheets from sweating all night. This was a new challenge and I wasn't fairing too well.

After about an hour of shivering and thinking warm thoughts, Mrs. Cathy came in to check on me. She saw that I was shaking and cold so she brought me another blanket. She put it right on top of me, plugged it into the wall and said, "That should do the trick." I was terrified when I saw her walking over to plug it in to the electrical socket! I was sure she was going to burn me up. I thought I was going to catch fire and I was so scared. But as I lay down under that blanket and felt the coils warm up, I was relieved. The warmth of that blanket made me sleep like a baby. I was so thankful for that heating blanket. All the coldness left me and I was warm again.

These kindsa things were new to me and I was scared by things I didn't know about, but at that moment I decided to put my ignorant attitude behind me. There were things I didn't know and I decided to put my Honduran mentality aside and to embrace the world I was living in.

"We are Family"

My California mother had a son named Ken who treated me so good. He loved me like a sister, taking me out with his friends and treating me so nice, like I belonged. I have two twins now that I named after my California brother; their names are Ken and Kenny. One time Ken and his friends had a party up there in the States and he took me along. This was my first party in the United States and it was a lot different than the parties I had been to. The party was full of people and Ken presented me to his friends as his adopted sister. I met a lot of girls and boys at that party and they were playing some crazy music. They took me up on the dance floor and I had no shame. This gringo guy had been drinking a bit and all he wanted to do was talk and dance with me. He asked me where I was from so I told him Honduras and he said, "Tell me Carolina, what's Honduras like?" Now I was feeling good myself and here is the joke, I said, "Honduras is Paradise!" I couldn't let my country down.

Many tourists come to my island now and to them this statement may seem true. They see the white beaches, beautiful resorts and friendly people, but my reality is and always has been very different. A look into my everyday life can be a painful and often wretched experience. There is a lot more to Roatan than the small piece of paradise.

French Harbour canal, Roatan   Turquoise Bay, Roatan

I made plenty of jokes that night, and they loved having me there. My dancing was different than theirs and they would ask me where I learned my moves. I told them, "I taught myself to dance." and I started teaching them some things. This one guy that was dancing with me was big and fat. We had all kindsa fun that night doing stupidness. I represented my country well that night with my dancing and with my descriptions of the place. No matter what my daily life looks like, I still have pride for where I come from. I told all of them, "When you drink the water of Honduras it will make you always want to come back; it's sweet like honey."

The Church

My California family also used to take me to the church, which wasn't new for me. I always went to church back on the island. I would go in the morning and in the evening; it's where I felt full. I have always loved church. It makes me feel happy, because I hear good things about the Lord, good music, positive preaching, and I love the fellowship with friends.

Sometimes I see people in church who I haven't seen in a long time and we get to worship together like no time has passed. Some people come and make friends with me that I don't even know. That's why I like the church, for the peace of God and for the fellowship. It's the biggest family in the world.

I used to be more faithful as a child. I feel like I am far away from God when I am close to my family. They take God for granted. I wake up and I hear F*** you being yelled from a porch or a child being beat. That ain't praising God. They curse around their kids and those words sink in. I heard a 3 year old boy the other day saying the 'F' word and cursing at his grandmother. He didn't even know what he was saying. Kids are like parrots, they just repeat what they hear. When you plant good seed you have good fruit; when you plant bad seed you have bad fruit. The darkness I live around pulls me away from God.

You know when I was younger I even used to be filled with the Holy Spirit and speak in tongues. Kevin, my oldest boy, used to always be praising in church too. He would sing and preach so loud they wanted to plug their ears but now he don't even want to see a church because he has fallen so far away from God. This place brings us down and Satan takes hold. I feel like a sinner right now, I need to do better with my life. I don't feel too close to God. My focus has been all on my boys and the problems. I believe I need to focus on myself for a while. I'm always worrying about them and never worrying about me. It's beginning to take a toll on me.

But no matter what happens, I always have God in my heart. I may fall away but He never leaves. God is faithful even when we are not. I have always been a part of the church and my time in California was no different.

I told Mrs. Cathy that I went to a Pentecostal church in Roatan so they found me a Pentecostal church in California. I was surprised that it was so much like my church at home. This is the one thing I had in the States that felt comfortable and familiar. The first time I went to church, I was shocked to see a familiar face. This woman ran up to me and started hugging me up and was so excited. I was asking myself who this lady was and why she was so excited. I thought maybe it's just the Holy Spirit makin' her crazy. Then I realized it was Mrs. Francis Arch's niece.

We called Mrs. Francis after church and told her that we had met up and she was so happy that I found someone I knew in the States. Not long after that I ran into Mrs. Francis' sister, Mrs. Betty. Throughout my time in the States, these two women constantly checked up on me and made sure I had all I needed. Church was a good place for me to go and keep myself busy but it was only two nights a week so Mrs. Cathy decided to put me in school to give me something to occupy the rest of my time.

I met all kindsa people in School, Puerto Ricans, whites, blacks, and others. It was fun to be in a place with such different types of people all learning together. While I was there I joined a club where I made a lot of friends. I can't remember now what the club was for but I made friends that I will never forget. I guess that is what was important, the friends I made. I remember us taking a picture while we held up a banner one day at school. I had that picture in my house for years and looked at it all the time but I can't even remember what the banner said. Sometimes what you are doing isn't the important part, it's who you're doing it with. That picture got burned up in the fire, but that was years later. Let me finish with my time in the States.

I was there, in the States for almost 6 months before I got my operation and then another 2 after the operation to recover. The doctors worked on me in the hospital and I was unconscious for seven hours. It was scary because I was only supposed to be out for four hours. The doctors and my family were scared because they didn't think I was going to wake up from the sleep. I thank God for His protection during my operation. When I finally did wake up, Glenda, Mrs. Betty's daughter, was right there standing with tons of flowers. They brought me gifts and all kindsa things that I wasn't used to and there was always somebody there for me in the hospital which made me feel special. At 18 years old, this is the best I was ever treated in my life and these people were practically strangers. I stayed for a while longer with Mrs. Cathy's family and for the first time in almost 7 years I was able to eat normal food. I was still on a special diet but it was normal food. I never thought I would eat like this again, but here I was with a full belly and a grin on my face

Church bus in French Harbour

Buen Provecho
(Enjoy your meal)

I had the surgery and it went perfect. They unlocked my jaw and told me to exercise it throughout the day to loosen up the joints even more. I woke up out of the 7 hour sleep and I felt perfect, I didn't even feel like they cut me. I had no idea where I was or what had happened, but eventually when I saw all the people around me, everything became clear. I thank God for all the help those Americans gave me. If I would have stayed the way I was, I would be a long time dead.

When I was recovering all I wanted to do was eat. I hadn't eaten real food in so long and it was exciting to finally enjoy the food I once knew. One day Mrs. Cathy asked me why I was sad and I told her it was because I wanted to eat but it wasn't dinner time yet and she told me to go on in the kitchen and make myself a sandwich. This was so new to me and I was shocked that she let me go into the kitchen on my own. Back on the island things weren't like this. The only time you went into the kitchen was if momma or grandmother asked you to come in and help.

Mrs. Cathy saw that this made me uncomfortable so she sat me down and explained that this is how things worked here and if I wanted something to eat, I could go in the kitchen and make anything I wanted. I took this as permission to make a meal. I made red beans, potato salad and spaghetti 'O's for the whole family that night. We all sat down to this meal I had prepared and everyone was so shocked by how good I cooked. I explained to them that this is how we cook and eat on the island all the time.

Right before I went to have my surgery, I had just started cooking for people to make a little money on the side. I had learned to cook just by watching other people. I was usually cleaning dishes or cleaning floors but I am very observant so I just watched everything the cooks did. When they saw that I was interested, they began to teach me a few things and before I knew it, I was regularly cooking meals for entire families. This is how I learned to cook good meals like I made Mrs. Cathy and her family that night.

Carolina after a writing session

A Family Apart

Before I left Honduras to go to the States, I had gotten in touch with my mom and told her that some Gringos were taking me up to give me an operation. She was living in New York at the time and would always write me letters and send a little money for my

31

grandmother to take care of me. My mother was good to me that way. Some mothers just leave their children and forget about them completely, but my mom never forgot about me. She wasn't with me but she cared for me the best she could. She would write to me every month to tell me how she was doing and to send us a few dollars that she could spare but the money didn't matter. What mattered is that she remembered me.

She was a loving mother and I appreciate everything she taught me. There is no love like a mother's love. I pray one day that my own children will understand that. I hope they will be able to read this book and see how I felt about my mother. Maybe someday they will express something like that for me too.

Children don't realize the sacrifices made for them and how a mother gives herself up for them. I don't blame my mother for leaving me with my grandmother. My daddy gave her a hard life and she had no choice; she couldn't stay there and be tortured. She had to leave and find love on her own just like me. How could she love me or anyone else if she had no love for herself?

I planned to meet up with my mother in New York after my operation, but we never had the opportunity. The whole trip was planned out and we talked a lot about it on the phone but one day I got a terrible call from my sister in New York. My mother, Angela Bennett died at the age of 46 in 1981. I did end up going to New York and being with my family for the funeral. For the first time, I met my three older sisters and I spent a few days there with them getting to know their lives. Getting to know my sisters was one of the happiest times of my life. It's ironic because of the circumstances but I believe God works out all things for good and this was one time He was at work. I never saw my sisters again but I keep in touch with them by phone.

It was so good to meet my sisters on that trip to NY. We were able to catch up and truly get to know each other for the first time. My mother died and we were all very sad but without that funeral I may have never connected with my sisters. God brings good out of all circumstances. My mother's death brought a bond to the family that there had never been and that will never be taken from us.

All three of my sisters had been left here by my mother as well with other family and friends but they had hustled and hustled and hustled until they got to the States. Barbara Lopez, Wanda Miranda, and Marylin Cristales are my sisters and I appreciate them. I love them and always pray for them because they have been good to me. Barbara has been so faithful in helping me to provide for myself and my children. Wanda is a pastor and I always call her when I have problems with my kids. She takes it to God and everything calms down for me. Marylin is always there for me when I call and I appreciate the way she cares. May the blessings of the Lord always fall on them.

Carolina standing by her grandmother's grave

<u>Home?</u>

Soon after returning from the States in 1982, I moved back in with my cousin Jacqueline and my grandmother. I was about 19 years old when my grandmother began to get really sick. My grandmother was on her last breath. She raised Jacqueline and me since we were babies but she loved Jackie the most. My uncle built the house we lived in for my grandmother when he came from the States a long time before. When he came to build the house a few years before, he saw how I was living and he felt bad for me. I was in a rented room that was falling in on me. My uncle had compassion for me and he wanted to help me out too.

He saw how miserable it was for me to live in that rented room and he said that the house he built should go to me once my grandmother died. My uncle knew I needed it and he had loved my mother a lot so he wanted to make sure I was taken care of.

When my grandmother was dying, my Aunt Nora (Jacqueline's mom) kept telling her to give the house to Jackie. But my grandmother had made a promise to my uncle and she had to give the house to me so she could die in peace. I had nothing at this point in my life so this was all I had to hope for. All the rest of my cousins had land because their family had given it to them. My mom had gone up to the States and left everything in her sister's hands so I was on my own. Now I was about to get my piece. I am so thankful for my uncle's gift and his love for me.

My grandmother died in 1982 and kept her promise to give me her house on The Hill. I didn't move in immediately because I wanted to show respect for the dead. So I waited for a while to let things calm down. After some time had passed I rented it out to a Spanish couple and I moved to another part of French Harbour called the 'Point'.

Love Lost

Soon after I returned to Roatan I met Edmon Green. He was my first boyfriend. He was from La Ceiba but was visiting Roatan and I met him in the Disco. I used to go all the time, every time with a new suit on and everybody would grab me to go and dance. I felt like a new woman after the surgery, like I could do anything. Edmon and I were together for about 4 years but we never had any kids. He had a baby boy though from another lady. He would bring me the baby to take care of when he had to work or he had things to do.

People must have thought I was made to be a babysitter. They would always leave their babies with me and I would clean them up or take care of them because I have patience with babies and I show them love. I guess it is my gift. Edmon used to be with all kinds of girls and I didn't like that so one day I told him I was through.

We broke up and he went back to La Ceiba. After that, his father got his papers together and he went to the States. When we were together he didn't have a consistent job but he would do all the work around the house while I was working. He stayed with me and treated me real good. I would come home from work and he would tell me, "Babe, go in there and rest." He was the best man I was ever along with. He became a Christian after some time in the States and now he talks to me about the lord. He even sent me a Bible one time. He is still good to me even though we aren't together. He has sent me things I could never get here, like a camera and a Blackberry. I think he plays in a band now too and he is married with kids in the States. It's a good life Edmon has made up there. I am happy to have him as a friend.

Life Goes On

In 1985 my first son was born. His name is Kevin and he is the one that causes me the most trouble today. Two years later, my second son was born. His name was Augustito. In 1990 I was sick with Cholera and had just been taken to the hospital because I was getting worse and worse. I was in the bed tossing and turning one day when I heard the news that at the age of three, my son, Augustito had died. I was in the hospital for a few days before I was told anything; I loved my son Augustito very much! He would always be jumping on the bed so happy and full of energy. He was only three years old and I had named him after his Uncle Augusto.

When I went to the hospital, I had left my sons with my aunt Gladis, because their father was on the sea working. Kevin was about 5 years old and the baby was 3. They took me to the hospital and I left my boys there so happy, happy, happy. Four days later my cousin Jacqueline came to look for me in the hospital. I had not been able to sleep all night and I knew something was wrong.

When I looked at her walking in, I saw her with a sad face. I said to her, "Hello Jackie," and she kept looking at me so sad. I said, "What happened, Jackie?" She said, "I'm sorry to tell you." I said, "Sorry to tell me what." Then she finally told me, she said, "Augustito is dead." All I could do was say, "What???" I started screaming in that hospital. I went insane in there and I told that doctor, "Get me outta here today." They told me that my time was not up. I was going crazy and I said, "Time is not up? Time has to be up!" and I started pulling all the stuff out of my arms. I decided that I was going to get out myself. I told the doctor, "I have to go see my son. I have to get out of here." That's when Jackie told me the worst of it. She said, "You can't see him Carolina, we already buried him." I started going crazier and crazier. I was pulling my hair and screaming. Everyone knew they couldn't hold me no more because I was a crazy woman in that moment and they said they were going to let me out.

Someone had just told me that my son had died! You can imagine how I felt. They let me leave but I didn't go with Jackie in a taxi because I couldn't bear to be with her. I couldn't take it. I didn't understand how they could do this to me. They came to tell me that my son was dead after they had already buried him.

So I left the hospital and I caught a taxi by myself. I didn't even make the taxi take me to my house. I made him stop straight at the graveyard gate. I looked all around for the first grave that I saw that was fresh and I went straight there because I knew it was my son. **I lay down on that grave and I screamed my heart out.** I fell down on that grave and faded away. The next thing I knew someone was shaking me awake.

My family came and found me fainted on the grave and they picked me up and took me home. I couldn't sleep or eat for days. Every morning at 5am I had to be there by that grave. I couldn't accept that it was my boy there in that grave. At least they could have tried to come and look for me, so I could see the last of my son. How could they bury my child without me? I couldn't accept it for a long time.

It was a shame how he died. The person who really told me about it was my aunt Gladis' son. He had just gotten out of jail and they called him Rambo. He said to me, "Prima (cousin), when I ran away from jail and I came home, I asked for you and they told me you were sick in the hospital. I saw the little boy and he was happy, as good as gold." Rambo said he could recall that my aunt had made some meat, some pork meat, and they fed him some. Maybe it wasn't cooked good enough or maybe he was allergic to something in it. They gave my little boy some of that meat, and he got very sick. He started vomiting. They could have saved his life at this point but they didn't pay him no mind. He was complaining and vomiting and they did nothing. He stayed that way for a couple days. No one cared for him or took the effort to carry him to the clinic 100 yards away. After a couple of days he began to turn kinda purple in the face and they finally decided to take him to the Centro de Salud (health clinic). My family did nothing for him until he was almost gone.

When my family got to the clinic, he was already fading away and there was nothing the doctors could do for him. They gave him some lime juice and other fluids but they couldn't do anything to save him. My son's life became like mine; nobody cared about him. When his mother wasn't around, no one cared for him. Nobody cares for you like your mother. The doctor said, "Why did you bring him so late, you should have brought him long ago?"

I wanted to give up my life when Augustito died, but then I realized that there was more to life than that because I had another kid; I couldn't give up. Life goes on. It took me a couple of years to get over my son's death; that was so hard for me. I wanted to end my life every day. For a few months I went to the grave twice a day, morning and evening. I started losing weight and losing my appetite but I decided that I have to be strong. I realized that he was gone but I know where he is. He is in God's hands. He was an angel. The Bible says to be happy when someone dies and be sad when someone is born, because you don't know what this world will bring upon them. But when someone dies they are at rest. I don't know if anyone has been through the type of tests I have been through and continue to face but I pray for those who have.

> *I been through some things, I tell ya. His daddy didn't get to see him nor his mother. These are the reasons I am writing this book about my life because I am talking about reality, not something somebody has told me. This is my reality, day to day. That's what I tell my boys. When they lose their mom they have lost everything. They don't realize it and they probably won't until I am gone. I tell them that but they don't pay it no mind. No one cares about you like your mother. You can have a million people like a father but only one mother. Only a mother can give you that love. No one can give it to you apart from her and Jesus. That's a mother's job here on earth, to love her kids and to show them the love of the Creator.*
> *-Carolina*

Made up Like a Preacher

      Two years after Augustito died, in 1992, I was living back on the Hill. The house my grandmother gave me was falling apart but it was my home so I did the best I could. My third son, Tyron, was born about this time. He is a hard worker when he wants to be but he has an attitude just like the rest of his brothers so it makes it hard for him to keep a job. When things don't go the way my boys want them to, you better step out of their way. They get full of anger and do stupid things without using their heads. Tyron makes me feel the best though. He is the one boy who always makes me feel special, like the way a mother should feel. He comes and wraps his arms around me and loves me real good like none of his other brothers.

      I named him after my brother, who I had never met but I wanted to honor him by keeping his name in our family. I finally did get to meet my brother a few years ago but it was not the type of meeting I had hoped for. My brother was visiting the island as a pastor from a church on the mainland. I had heard he was preaching at a local church so I went to meet him for the first time in my life. But when I saw him he didn't treat me how a brother should treat a sister or even how a pastor should treat another person.

      I didn't know what to expect when I went to meet Tyron because I had heard all kindsa stories about him. Some said he was a great preacher and others said he was a bad man. I heard this one story that his wife cheated on him and he had killed her. I don't know if it is true but I know he spent some time in prison in the States and then was sent him back to Honduras even though he was a U.S. citizen. So he became a preacher in Honduras, but when I met him he had turned his back on God.

I named my son Tyron after my brother thinking he was a good man. I sent my son Tyron to go and meet his uncle down by Gio's restaurant while he was visiting the island because I think family should know each other. But when my son got down to the restaurant, his uncle pushed him aside and acted like he didn't want to see him. He treated my son like he was a piece of trash.

He was on the island for a while and never came by the house or even acknowledged us. He didn't give us nothing. He even made me a promise before he left. He promised to send some groceries from the mainland because they were a lot cheaper there. That was an empty promise; he never did anything for us.

I told my sisters how he had treated us and they said, "That's just how he is. He is selfish; that's how he treats all of us." I regret naming my boy after him, and it's funny how this works because my son Tyron can act just like his uncle sometimes. I guess the name fits. He can be so selfish sometimes and doesn't want to help out with his own family. My brother Tyron is black like me and he is my blood but he thinks he's not. He thinks he is better than the rest of us. He gets all dressed up as a preacher and forgets where he comes from, and his reason for preaching. We are all from the same mother and we need to stick together. My sisters treat me good but my brother acts like he doesn't know me.

My one and only brother, Tyron Brown, wherever you may be, God be there with you. You don't care for nobody but I still pray that God will lead you.

-Carolina

"Mi Casa, No Su Casa"

After my grandmother died, I was living on the Hill and I had so many problems with the people there. I had no peace where I was living so I rented the house to this Spanish couple and I moved to the Point. The Point is still in my town of French Harbour but it's far enough away to be separated from the drama of my family. I rented out a small apartment from the Collins family with one room and a place to cook outside. I wasn't working anymore but I found happiness and peace there because I was around a bunch of Christian people. We went to church together and if anyone needed anything we took care of each other. This is the only place where I have found peace during my life in French Harbour.

The Collins family took good care of me. They gave me cheap rent and helped me to sell the things I would bake. I used an old mud oven outside to bake buns, Johnny cakes, banana cake, roasted peanuts, and coco bread. After I baked I would send out Kevin to sell these things on the street. I would even fry pastels and burgers to sell and make a little extra money. Sometimes I would have nothing to eat, but I had good neighbors there that would come and provide food for my kids and I. I didn't like being in need all the time so I would try and get creative with ways to make money. This is when I started to do the raffles or try and sell a little bit of anything.

I sold everything from beer and candy to clothes and toys but I quickly realized that selling the clothes was the best way for me to make my money. I saved up about 1,500 lempiras ($80) and bought one pack of clothes to start selling out of my house. Sometimes I would have some white friends that would clean out

42

their houses and give me their kid's old clothes. Other times I would buy the big packages of clothes that were shipped here from the States. I still don't know how those clothes made it all the way to Roatan, but they are here and that's how I make a living. I've been making money that way ever since. I moved to different apartments at the Point but stayed in that area for about 7 years, until 1999.

The last apartment I lived in was a bad experience. The owner kept raising the rent on me and he would always be late paying the light bill so Roatan Electric Company (RECO) came and cut off the lights on a regular basis. Electricity has long been a problem on the island for us. RECO provides the electricity for 70,000 people. They burn over 20,000 gallons of diesel fuel a day and it costs us about 19 times the cost of power in the States.

The owners of the apartment couldn't keep up with the bills so RECO would come and cut off our lights and we were left there living in the dark for days. I talked to my neighbors who were living in the same building and we decided to pay for our own lights from RECO. I told them not to use the iron because it would make the light bill go up higher. The bill kept going up and up and up. Then I would show them the bill and they would start to complain that they didn't have the money this month. I became the bill collector because the lights were in my name and the burden would fall on me. After they didn't pay a couple of times I told them that they didn't have to pay the bill but I was going to cut them off of the electricity. I decided to figure out a way to pay it on my own but I had to cut them off because they were running me into the ground.

I cut them off, hustled up some money and paid the bills myself. After that, the owner saw that I had bought all the cable and connections for the lights and he wanted to use me like a fool. He said, "When you leave from here I want to pay you for all the equipment you bought." I said, "Who told you I was going to sell it?

Wherever I go I am going to need this equipment." He took me for a fool but I am a wise girl. When he saw that I wasn't going to give in he started to raise the rent on the house. He made me pay more for water and rent. So I told him, "Give me a month and I will be moving out."

I planned to move back to the Hill because the Spanish couple was moving out. They were constantly having trouble with my family who lived around them. I had no renters and my rent was going up so I had to go back to the house. This is the reason I didn't want to move into the house. I know my family and their ways. Because my Aunt didn't get what she wanted, she was going to make sure whoever stayed in that home would live in constant torment and regret for moving there. I moved in and have been tormented for having what's mine every day since. I have been fighting every day since for my rights, to be in my own home. I have to stand for what's mine every minute or it will be taken from me. I remain firm in my home even though my family wants to fight, fight, fight all the time. There is no peace around my home.

When I moved back into the house, Nora was the one giving me all kindsa trouble. One day Nora and Jackie got in a fight and Jackie came to me crying out, "I am going to chop her with a machete." Jackie grabbed a machete, went back to her mother's house, and took a swing at her but hit the door. If Nora hadn't ducked, the machete would have hit her right in the head. Jackie went in and got all her stuff from Nora's house and came to my house begging to put her things in there and stay with me because she couldn't go home. I said no because I knew if I let her get into my house, I would never get her out.

This may sound a little heavy, but its normal behavior for the place I live on the Hill. Anger and violence are natural and acceptable for everyone around me. Men beat their wives, wives beat their kids, kids beat other kids and the cycle continues. Violence is a way of life here.

My aunt Nora would curse me every day for living in the house she believed wasn't mine. She made my life miserable there but I stood my ground. She would beat on the walls early in the morning, throw dirty water under the floorboards, tell lies about me, and leave trash all over my property.

People are funny though; she would do all these things to me but then pretend like none of it was happening when we were in public together. My time in that house was miserable, not only because of my family but also because the house was falling apart all around us. My only possession of any value was deteriorating before my eyes and there was nothing I could do about it.

By this time I had my next son. His name is Theron but everyone knows him as Bebe. He was born in 1995 and has always been the closest to me. He is 16 now and always stays by my side when things get tough. When my family saw that they were not going to move me, they began to calm down. If everyone would fight for their rights they would have their rights. If you fight for what is yours you will get it but if you give up you lose. You have to try somehow.

I was the black sheep of the family. No one wanted me to have anything, so I took what was mine.

New Hope

My home was decrepit and falling down around us. The boys and I lived in that house while it fell apart around us for five years. We would go to sleep at night and wake up to crabs crawling under our beds or water pouring in through the roof when it rained. Everything smelled because of the rotting floorboards and the marshy ground underneath the house. I was not happy in that place for a long time but I accepted it as a blessing from God. I had a house while many other people in the world have nothing. I accepted it as a blessing but I didn't stop trying to improve our circumstances.

One day I was sitting by my house and I heard that Jerry Hinds was up by the Hill working on a project for the government. He became Alcalde (Governor) of the island that year, in 2004, and he was always around our community doing work. I went out on the road that day and found Jerry to ask him a favor. I knew Mr. Jerry would help me out because I have known him since I was a little girl. I didn't ask him to give me anything at first I simply asked that he would stop by my house to see where I lived before he was finished for the day. He gave me his word that he would stop by for a few minutes later that day.

After a couple of hours he called me and said, "Let's go." We walked down the Hill, me and him, and I took him straight to my house. A lot of people wanted to ask him for help when they saw him in French Harbour that day but they were 'shamed. I wasn't 'shamed of nothing. As long as I don't steal, I am not 'shamed to ask for help when I need it. I took him to my house and asked him if he could help me get materials to fix my roof and floors. I wasn't asking him for much, just some wood and some aluminum. What I got was a lot more than a few materials!

When Jerry came to the house I had three of my little boys bathing, the walls were all torn up and there was water under the house with mosquitoes and crabs everywhere. I guess his heart became full when he saw my situation. He said, "Carolina, if you never brought me here, I would never have known you were living in a mess like this." He said, "I want to help you. Give me a little time and I will see what I can do for you."

When he said that, he gave me hope. So I decided every time I would see him I would remind him not to forget me. Sometimes I would wait outside of Gio's restaurant and remind him of his word. He would say, "OK Carolina, I am working on it, just keep reminding me." Wherever I would find him, I would keep reminding him, just like the woman in the Bible who goes to the judge over and over again until he finally gives her what she needs. If you want something, or need something, you must be persistent. One day I found him and he said, "I think I will be able to help you soon. I have one piece of land that I am about to sell and when that happens I will be able to build you a brand new house."

Jerry Hinds with Carolina today

He called me soon after that and said, "Go get some of those drug boys that live there on the Hill and have them come to break down the house. They can take any of the materials they want, we are bringing new things." I began to praise the Lord because my prayers were being answered. These boys off the street came and broke down the house and got everything cleaned up for me.

Within minutes my aunt was yelling all kindsa stupidness. She was shocked when she saw them tearing down my house. She said to this guy, "They will never build her a house. They are lying to her. Carolina will never see that house go up."

One day I ran into Jerry and I told him what she and other people were saying. He looked at me and said, "Carolina, what Jerry says, Jerry will do." And I tell you, that is a man of his word.

About 2 weeks later people were shocked. They saw truckloads of materials being brought in and dropped off. Nobody could believe that it was really happening. Then the workers started to show up and lay the foundation. They were measuring, leveling the ground and pouring concrete. I was so happy to see Jerry's promise coming to pass.

My aunt had been stealing my land over the years by putting fences up and all so my piece of land was small and right down in the mud. They were measuring for the house, and Nora started to tell the workers to move the house further out. She was trying to steal more of my land. The Spanish workers all got scared and they stopped the job. When I saw everyone sitting around by the house I said, "What happened, why did the work stop?" They told me that my aunt wasn't letting them build and I asked the carpenter, "What happened to you, are you scared of her? Are you not a man? Call Jerry and let me talk to him." So Jerry called the surveyor and he came with papers and a computer. Then he took the measurements and told Nora there was nothing she could do because the land was mine. Erick McKenzie built that house for me and I told him, "Put my house right back where it was, no mas no menos (no more, no less), right where it was."

They brought 2 police cars to stay there until the foundation of the house was laid. She couldn't do anything but she stayed there going on and on calling all of us crooks and saying they were all on my side. She told them not to put a window on her side of the house. She tried to control everything. They were scared of her but I told them that I wanted my windows there. It was my house and I wasn't going to have a house without windows. Jerry told them to build the house just how I wanted it so I stayed there and told them how to build it. She made all kindsa accusations against me, like I was along with Jerry and all this craziness. No one had trouble with me getting a house except her. She was the only one that caused me trouble.

Within weeks, my house was up!

So they built me that first house in 2004 and again I was at peace for a while. My family still treated me bad but we were able to live with less problems. Four years later, in 2008 a terrible fire came through French Harbour. 15 or 16 houses got burned up all around me but mine stayed standing. After the fire, everyone began going to the Alcalde but that Governor was not too good for them. I didn't have faith in him. These people were going to have to rebuild themselves. My house was spared in that fire but my luck soon ran out.

A few months later, my son Tyron was in the house by himself using a candle to see because it was dark. He heard his friends calling him from the street so he left real fast, forgetting to put out the candle. The candle was lit with the door shut and nowhere for the heat to go. I came walking up the street to see my home in flames.

Tyron tried to lie to us at first because he was so scared and worked up but he couldn't lie to us because we all knew he was the last one in the house. He felt so sad and I was full of anger for a while. I didn't know what to do. I said, "Oh Lord, here I am on the street again, but still I didn't lose faith."

When my house burned down, I had no place to go so I made a plastic tent on my property next to the ashes of my house. It was a terrible time. The crabs would come in at night and when it would rain we were constantly plugging holes and throwing off water. We would wake up every morning with pain in our bones and weary from no sleep. The boys would sometimes go and stay at a friend's house, but I had nowhere to go. This was home for now. I had to figure out another way.

Jerry Hinds never stopped caring for me after he built me that house. Every time I would see him, he would give me a little something. He would always give me a little money to buy food and things for my kids.

About two months after my house burned down Jerry came and did what I thought would never be possible. He came and rebuilt my house. I told him on the street one day what had happened and asked if he could help. I was shocked by his giving heart again. He sent his guys over to start the building and this time they made the house even better. They raised it up about six feet on stilts so that I would be up away from the bugs and so that I could have storage under my house. My aunt Nora came out when they were building and caused the same trouble as before but I think they knew how to handle her this time. Once again I was praising God for always providing and I was doing my best to appreciate Mr. Jerry.

I don't ask Jerry for things anymore because he has done so much for me. I just wish there was something I could do to repay the good that he has done for me. I am always thankful for him and I tell my kids to always respect him. I pray that God will always bless him.

Carolina's second house built by Jerry Hinds

Jobs

When I was still a teenager, I learned how to bake, cook, wash clothes and how to clean houses just by watching everybody around me and letting them teach me. One time I made a mistake in Mrs. Lena McNab's house. I was mopping the floor and then walking in all the clean places. She was so frustrated with me because I would mop one side, and then start the other and I would dirty it all up again. She taught me that you are supposed to mop while backing up to keep the floor clean while it dries. She said, "Carolina if you are going to learn to clean, you are going to learn with me. I can't have you wasting your time by mopping the same place every day. Now you need to mop this floor

51

again the right way." I put on a smile and mopped it again, the way she taught me. Most people would have gotten mad if they had to do the same work twice but I considered that part of my education. I have always loved to learn; when you stop learning you stop living. If I was going to be good at anything I had to listen to people who knew better than me.

Mrs. Lena taught me lotsa' things. One time she asked me to babysit for her, so I went over to take care of her child. This was the first time anybody had every paid me to watch a kid. Usually people just put their kids in my lap and walked off. I would sit there with somebody's child for hours and sometimes they would return without even saying thank you. I was rocking Mrs. Lena's baby that day and trying to get her to fall asleep. I must have been rocking too good though because before I knew it, the baby and I were both asleep. The baby was in my arms as I rocked in that chair and we were both sound asleep.

Mrs. Lena came in and yelled at me so hard because she said I could have dropped her baby. She yelled at me that day and I learned my lesson, but it is so funny looking back on it now because sometimes the child is so peaceful, you get tired too. But she was right. I could have dropped her child that day. I was always good with kids but Mrs. Lena taught me how to really care for them. There were several houses I learned at but that is the house where I learned to clean and that's the child I learned to care for.

I got good at these things and people would call me all the time to come clean their houses. They were all the time praising me for cleaning their houses. They would pay me 50 lempiras ($2.50) a month. In 1981 that was a lot of money; like it would be 1,000 lempiras ($52) now. Some of the houses I cleaned before I went to the States and some I cleaned after I came back. I did this type of work for a long time, even after I had my boys.

The last time I had a job cleaning was for a real estate company about 3 or 4 years ago. Sometimes my kids would like to come with me to work but the real estate people didn't like that so I lost some of those jobs. The last job I had, the lady didn't like the way I cleaned so she told me to stop cleaning. After that I decided that I had been killing myself working for people and I figured its better now that I work for myself! So I saved up my money and I bought one pack of clothes to sell. The clothes are shipped here from the United States, like from Goodwill and other places. For a big bundle of clothes, it costs about 2,000 lempiras ($106). I give my kids some clothes and I sell the rest. That has been my living for years now.

One day, I was just sitting at my house trying to sell some clothes and this white woman comes running up to me so excited and talking real fast. I had no idea who this crazy woman was at first but once she started talking, I realized it was Mrs. Amy, the woman from Stanford who helped me get to the States. I wanted to know her because she had helped me so much but I didn't think it would ever happen until that day 13 years ago. She told me who she was and that she was only visiting the island for the day on a cruise ship, and that she had wanted to see me.

I was shocked and I felt so loved. She had found a taxi and paid him to drive her around Roatan all day until she found me. Ms. Amy asked and asked and asked until she found me here in French Harbour, down by the Point. She found me there with my two babies lying on the bed, and she was so excited I thought she was going to eat me. She said, "Oh Carolina I was looking all over this island for you!" She left me with all kindsa things from the States and everyone was saying, "Look at how that lady loves Carolina." She loved me real good and I knew she cared about me that day. I am glad I got to meet this woman who changed my life by living hers.

I have tried to do the same thing with my life. I sit on the street most days selling clothes or anything else I have and I try to be a blessing to everyone I see. I interact with people in every job so it gives me an opportunity to share my life with them and I hope something good comes of it.

I have had a lot of other odd jobs as well. When you live in a place like this, you learn to do whatever you can to survive. We all gotta eat and we all gotta live. I already spoke of my job at the Yacht Club when I was 14. It was very difficult because of my disability but I still served tables and cleaned rooms. I worked there for about 3 years.

Some years back I used to take things and raffle them on Sunday's. I stopped doing that about 5 years ago. I would put the numbers on slips of paper and sell the numbers. Then I would draw one out at the end of the week to see who won whatever I was raffling. I wasn't making very much money and sometimes I was even losing money. Like say I was raffling 1,000 lempiras and I didn't sell enough tickets, I realized that I was losing more than I was winning. So after a little while I stopped the raffles and I went back to selling clothes.

I always try to work because I like paying my bills and I don't like owing people money. I always work to have enough. If I don't have enough I just stop and go without so I don't have to owe someone. One bill that I always make sure I pay is my light bill. I have never had them come to me and try to cut off my lights. I have always been faithful with my light bill. I don't believe in crediting nothing just to have it look beautiful. I believe that if God wants me to have something He will provide it. I will not be upset if you get something and I don't. I am happy with what I have. Some people get things and then try to rub it in someone else's face and that's wrong. If God wants me to have something He will give it to me. There is a true word that says 'good things come to those who wait' and I am a waiter.

Kendall and Carolina sitting on the street selling clothes

Begging for the Broken

One thing I used to do for work was to beg. I
didn't have nothin' for my family, so I would go up by
Eldon's Supermarket to beg. I would stand there all day
begging for the kids. My one son, Kevin, was the oldest
and he worked all the time in restaurants and hotels or

55

making music. He was a singing artist but he would take all his money straight to the Hill to buy drugs. Then he would come home and eat that same food I begged for. Sometimes I would go home with 100 lempiras ($5), sometimes 400 lempiras ($20) and sometimes nothing. People would be insulted by me and say mean things while I begged for my family. They would tell me to get a job but they didn't understand my situation. When I would stand for a long time, my legs would swell up. I eventually got fed up with it and said, "I'm not going to do this anymore." I decided that my kids are big enough and they should be providing for me. So many days I went hungry! But if I was hungry then the kids were hungry and they would eventually learn that if we were going to survive, we all had to work.

One day, Kevin came home and I had all the pots on the stove like I was cooking a big meal. He came home and went straight to the kitchen but found only water in the pots. He said, "What's this, I am hungry! Where is the food?" I said, "You are a grown man! It's your job to provide for this family too. I have been begging and begging and these people are looking down on us. You should be taking care of us, not throwing your money away." He had just gotten paid about 4,000 lempiras and the night before he went and spent it all partying and using cocaine. He would always come in and the first thing he would do was to check the pots for food. So I decided to set a trap for him that day. I wanted to teach him a lesson. But sometimes people don't listen.

Now he wants to take me out of my own house and he didn't put a nail in that house. He has been beatin' up on his little brothers and he has forced me to sleep on the street some nights because he treats us so bad. He has taken over my house and caused me to live in a state of torment. I worked the hardest for that one child. I even stole for the first time for that child. I stole milk from my job for him when he was a baby because I didn't have any for him. And now he is the one who treats me the worst.

He tells me that I don't care for him and he treats me bad. He is sick in the head I tell ya! He needs a doctor for his brains but I will always be praying for him. He has a lot to beg God's forgiveness for because you are not supposed to say hurtful things to your mother. I hopped on my cripple foot, working to keep him going as a child and that's the thanks I get. I don't speak to him right now because I have nothing to say to him. I have to be hard with him right now. Maybe he will get on his own, maybe he will change. He is 25 and needs to be on his own, not taking advantage of his mother. The Bible says to leave your mother and father and to be with a wife. He needs to marry and shack up with some girl but he keeps holding me down.

That is one of my biggest problems right now! I have all my boys sucking the life out of me and no one pouring life back in. I am 49 and my health is not too good. I have 5 boys from 14 years old to 25 and I am still taking care of them all. They have not set out on their own. They have decided to stay here and smother me. Don't get me wrong, I love my kids but at some point they have to grow up and start to be men, or at least help keep us afloat.

My other boys are 14, 15 and 20. They don't treat me as bad as Kevin but they are still dragging me down. They could easily follow in their brothers footsteps. They all have problems with anger and they don't listen to nobody. Just the other day I told my son Kenny not to go out on the street because he would get into trouble, but he didn't listen to his mother. A few hours later I got a call from the jail. Kenny had been arrested for harassing a security guard and was locked up for the night. He begged me to come and get him out but I refused. He is only 14 years old but maybe this will teach him a lesson. He needs to learn to respect authority and to respect his mother.

All my boys are lazy. Ken and Kenny have stopped going to school and they are just sitting at home all day or out on the street getting in trouble. They haven't gotten jobs and they don't care about their education. Bebe is still in school but it's a struggle everyday to make sure he is going to class. He is in 9th grade and will finish in the public school this year. Tyron is out of school and works a part-time job but he doesn't make enough money to support us and they don't always need him to work. They all have good hearts but they are all lazy and when there is nothing to keep them busy, they get into trouble. I am tired of pushing them up a hill that never levels out.

My Boys

Kevin is my oldest boy and like I said, he gives me the most trouble right now. While he was growing up, he was a great kid; he actually wanted to be a preacher. When we would go to church he would sing the loudest and people would praise him for his worship. He wanted to be a preacher when he was young but at some point the street got a hold of him.

Now Kevin makes money working or singing his songs but he holds his money back from me and spends it in the street. When things get real bad and I beg him enough he will give me a little bit but I shouldn't have to beg from my own kids; they are eating the food too. He also treats me and the other boys so bad when he is at home. He beats up on the younger boys and doesn't even let them sleep in the house some nights. If they have something he wants he takes it from them and if they say the wrong thing to him, he will beat them up. He curses me out sometime and says things to me that no mother should ever hear. He tells me I am worthless and that he doesn't owe me nothing.

The other day I came home and was locked out of my own house. My boys came and told me how Kevin had made them all leave. Then he took some girl from the street into my bedroom. He finally came out later that day and when I went into my room, the sheets were all wet and there were beer cans everywhere. He brought some random girl from the street into my bed. He has no respect for his mother, after all the things I have done for him. I am out of options. I don't know what to do except pray for God to help me out. It's such a shame, because I remember him telling me he wanted to be a preacher when he was a kid and I would get so excited about his future. My hope for my kids is that they would be good people and that they would be somebody. Now as I look at Kevin, I don't know what happened. I know he has a good heart, but he has lost his way so I pray for him. I think God can still use him.

My other boys are a little younger but they could easily follow in their brother's footsteps. They all have problems with anger and they don't respect authority. Kenny was locked in jail because he didn't respect that security guard, Bebe has gotten himself into too much trouble because he lets his anger drive him not his head and Ken won't take advice from anyone! He has too much pride. I always believe, if you do something wrong, it's wrong, and you should be punished for it. I won't even stand up for my kids. If I know what they are doing is wrong, they need to be punished. They all know right from wrong, I taught them that, and if they don't do what is right, they will get what they deserve.

I love my boys and I want the best for them. Bebe is in 9th grade and will soon graduate. I want to see him become somebody. He is the only one of my boys who has stayed in school this long and I see that he could really do something good but he is surrounded by all this darkness just like the rest of us. I pray for him because it's hard here, when you are trying to do something good. Everyone here on the Hill is so negative and they don't want to see you succeed, so you have to fight for it. That's why I pray for Bebe and I encourage him. It's easy to fall into the darkness without someone pushing you out.

My son Bebe

The other day my pressure went up so high and I thought I was going to die. I looked up to God and I said, "It's me again and I need your help." You can do whatever you want but my kids still need me, so I am asking you to make me feel better. I lay down again and I said, "I feel so bad I don't know if I can get back out of this bed but I believe God is good and He is going to do something." Tyron's heart got full and he called his brothers together to pray around me. Ken is the only one who didn't like it. I taught my kids that. When one of us is sick, we would always get together and pray for that one to get better, and we have faith that God will heal us. That worked for us and we always got better because we had faith and believed. They came around me and prayed and I woke up the next morning feeling stronger. I was so happy that Tyron remembered that thing from when he was little.

Pray For Us

I truly love my kids and I want the best for them but it gets hard on me. I am raising 5 boys to become men when there is no man around for them to see. I don't blame them 100% for the way they act. It is because of our environment. There is no man in our house to set an example, so any example they see of a man is out on the street. They believe what this dark world around us tells them which is; "Life is all about getting what you want and it doesn't matter who you step on in the process. "

This is why I appreciate the people in the church who know me and are able to come into this dark community to shine God's light. Most people have no hope for kids like mine but I do, and these people of God do as well.

I believe God has a plan for all of my kids and I am praying for them continually. They want to do good and they know how to do good, but they face a constant struggle against the darkness of drugs, sex, and violence which saturates this island.

I am writing this book because those things are real, here and everywhere. Satan has a hold in this world and we are constantly standing against it. I want people to know my story because I see the battle day to day. It is real; this is my life.

In the End God has victory. Pray for us.

Carolina, walking home

Afterward

A Gringo's Take

- By Harrison Johnson

I left my life behind in 2009 to find a place that I will never understand and people that I will never forget. My heart was full of excitement and passion to change the world as I landed in Roatan, Honduras on August 12, 2009. I entered what I like to call 'a beautiful mess'. My first year on the island was spent living in what was considered to be one of the "worst" towns called Los Fuertes or "The Strong Ones." Other Americans quickly identified dangers in the vicinity by saying things like, "Don't walk down that street!", "Don't trust the locals." or "Don't go there at night." What I quickly realized is that for the most part these Americans just feared what they did not understand. The local people who lived around me were full of more life and love than most Americans I have met here.

I call the island a beautiful mess because that's exactly what it is. Roatan is a beautiful island with a mess of people from all different backgrounds. Most of them are trying to survive with very little resources, organization or infrastructure. The population has doubled from 30,000 to almost 70,000 since the 80's and the Government couldn't seem to keep up. Thousands of people came, and are still arriving, to build a life in places with no more space. The areas without infrastructure are dirty, smelly and ugly, but many of the people who live there are full of life. They have nothing by North American standards but are willing to give and share out of their poverty. I have been humbled and blessed by the people of Roatan more times than I can count. A gift of fresh fish, shrimp, a bootleg Rolex, a coke, or an ice cream may seem menial or silly but for me these gifts have meant more than any 'Gift Card' ever will.

Poverty is everywhere on the island but it is rarely seen by the visitors who come to Roatan. They see the fancy resorts and the multi-million dollar golf course but they don't see the people that live on the other side of the cement wall. They don't see the family of 8 living in one room without a bathroom or the 13 year old boy who begs for every meal because he has 11 siblings and no fit parent to care for him. There is plenty of money on the island but like most of the world, it is in the hands of a few. The rich are not to blame and neither are the tourists. It is simply the reality. We live in a broken and messy world.

I have been immersed in the culture of this island and gotten to know the people. In doing so I cling to the hope I have in Christ. He is the only way and He is the only hope. I cannot face such an ugly reality without the knowledge and hope of an eternity with God. This dark world cannot be the final chapter.

This is where I find the beauty in the mess. God has made each person in Roatan and He made this island. It is His and He loves it. The white islanders, the black islanders, the Spanish, the Garifuna and the foreigners; He loves them all.

For my first few months, I drifted through life on the island. I taught my classes at a school, I explored new places and I hung out with the other American teachers. This quickly became monotonous and unfulfilling. This was not the life I came to discover. I spent hours praying at night for God to reveal his purpose for me here and for Him to lead me. Over the next few weeks, my purpose began to show up on my door step. God can be pretty direct when He wants something out of you. Three young girls began to show up at our apartment every day selling donuts and other miscellaneous things to make money for their families. The girls would come over and spend the afternoon with us playing silly games, drawing, and helping us to learn

Spanish. For a few hours a week they were able to be kids rather than vendors. My heart began to break for the kids of this island who are robbed of their childhood. The reality is that 70% of the kids in Roatan do not attend school and many of the ones that do attend receive a mediocre education. Many of the kids are forced to work in order to survive. Others simply choose not to go because they see no value in education, and no one is there to encourage them.

Not long after the girls began to show up at our apartments, I met a group of boys who would change my life. I met three boys begging on the street. Pablo approached me with his rehearsed lines and million dollar smile expecting a few bucks or a hot meal. The kids I met can read people like a book and have what a friend of mine calls a "Gringo Radar." If they can get something out of you, they know it and know how to get it. Pablo, Jorvick and Menfi approached me that night making jokes and capturing my heart within moments. They left with money for dinner and a new friendship that would go much deeper than a handout.

Kids from French Harbour

Two years later, those girls have a new home that was donated and built by generous Americans, and the boys are part of a growing mentoring program that provides education, job training and life skills. My role in all this has come from nothing more than loving the people in front of me. That's what brought me to this book as well. One of the boys I met through Pablo is

Bebe. He quickly began to shine in our mentoring program and insisted that I meet his mom. I was welcomed like family by his mother, Carolina. She opened up her house to me and shared her life, faith, and dreams with me. She told me that she had two dreams for her life. One was to become a missionary and the other was to write a book.

I didn't think much of what she told me that day until she handed me a stack of papers a few months later. She had spent hours writing the story of her life on loose sheets of notebook paper. The papers were all mixed up, some stained and torn, but they were all there. Her dream to share her story was to become a reality.

She handed the papers to me and asked if my wife and I would be willing to help her write it in English. The result is the story you have just read, her dream come true.

La Isla de Roatan

The place where Carolina grew up is Roatan. It is an island, 30 miles long and 4 miles wide in the western Caribbean. It would seem like an easy place to get around but that's not the case. The hills can be seen from mainland Honduras 30 miles away and the only road on the island curves and loops through the peaks and valleys from one end to the other. This forces drivers to go slow; it can take about 2.5 hours to get from one end to the other. Most of the locals don't have cars so their only means of transportation is in a taxi. But if someone can't put food on the table, they can't pay for a taxi ride. The poor, like Carolina don't leave home often.

The history of the island is very complex. The original people of Roatan were Mayan and Payan Indian tribes. You can still find artifacts on the island and hear stories of their gods and ceremonial rituals. In early colonial times the population of the island grew with slaves and pirates. The slaves were left here by European traders en route to the new world and the pirates came on their own accord. The groups of slaves who acted out and refused to obey were considered worthless; they could not be tamed. The traders were fed up with them and left them to fend for themselves here in Roatan. They established themselves, created their own culture, their own language and became island people. They are the Garifuna people. The Garifuna populated the Eastern portion of Roatan and lived off of the land and the sea, which are both rich in resources. The island is surrounded by the second largest coral reef in the world and the tropical climate is ripe with fruits and vegetables.

The sea and land have always provided for the people of the island in abundance until recently. Over the past 20 years, the sea has been over fished, the land has been privatized and the animals such as Iguana's and Watusi ('island rabbits') have diminished. At one time you could dive right off of the beach for conch and lobster or grab an iguana out of any nearby tree but now they are protected and rarely seen. The island culture is still alive today but can only be seen in the smaller communities. It has been slowly stripped away from them because of early British influence and today's ever expanding Westernization.

There have been multiple conquests by the Europeans and the Spanish throughout Roatan's history. The island was under their control for long periods of time. During all of Roatan's early years, the pirates had a say in these conquests. There were many problems between the Europeans and the pirates who would wreak havoc on their colonies and incoming ships. But ultimately the Europeans prevailed and their descendants are still very alive today in Roatan.

Even though Roatan is officially a part of Honduras, many of the islanders don't consider themselves Hondurans. An unspoken tension exists between the 'islanders' and the mainland Hondurans because of this. Much like the problems in the States, the mainland Hondurans have come to the island and taken most of the jobs. They are willing to work harder for less money. Fishing has always provided work for the locals but within the past 20 years, tourism has taken over. It is no longer possible for the locals to live like they always have so they have been forced to adapt. With the change in population and the influx of mainland Hondurans, the dominant language has shifted as well. Spanish is now more widely spoken but most people in Roatan are bilingual. You can find English and Spanish everywhere you go.

Roatan is rich in history and culture. If you came to here today, you would see, white islanders descended from the Europeans, black islanders whose descendants are from other parts of the Caribbean, Spanish from the mainland, Garifuna, Indio who are descended from the Mayans and many North Americans and Europeans who have come here to retire or get a taste of somewhere new. The island is a mix of people from all over and in reality it's a mess of people just trying to survive. It is filled with people just like Carolina Brooks.

She is a black islander, her first language is English but she only learned to read and write in Spanish because that is what the public schools teach. Her great grandfather was from Jamaica. He came to this island and fell in love with a girl from a town called Flowers Bay.

If you have been touched by her story, extend your generosity to Carolina by recommending her book to others who can benefit by reading the insights of an impoverished existence and gaining an understanding of the desperate needs on Roatan. If you are able, please visit our island by plane or cruise ship, and deposit some spare funds around the island wherever you see a real

need! This will bring further hope out of the despair
many face ... in The Darker Side of Paradise!

Compiled and Edited by:
Harrison Johnson
Kendall Johnson and
Pastor Bob Cowan

Support The Island:

Crafts
Check Out "Made in Roatan" to directly support local artisans. All profits go to the local islanders who make the products you see on the website.

www.made-in-roatan.com

Health
Clinica Esperanza is a Non-profit medical clinic in Roatan that provides top notch care to the locals for minimal to no cost. Please check out the website and support proper medical care for the local people.

www.clinicaesperanza.com

Community Development
Intensive Heart ventures reaches out to the local people by developing micro-enterprises, community development projects, emergency support and mentoring youth. Check out the website and support in any way you feel led.

www.heartventures.org

Children
There are two children's homes on the island of Roatan which are both in desperate need of volunteer teachers, mentors and finances. Please check out the following websites and pray about ways you may support.

www.csiroatan.org

http://www.roatanchildrenshome.com/

Made in the USA
Charleston, SC
24 November 2012